BROOKS *COMING HOME*

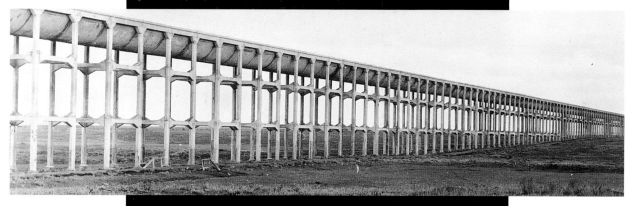

TEXT : WALTER HILDEBRANDT / IMAGES : PETER TITTENBERGER

Bayeux Arts
INCORPORATED

A GEORGE MELNYK BOOK

Brooks — Coming Home

Text : Walter Hildebrandt / Images : Peter Tittenberger
© Copyright 1996 by Bayeux Arts Incorporated

Published by :

Bayeux Arts Incorporated
119 Stratton Crescent S.W.
Calgary, AB, Canada T3H 1T7

P.O. Box 586
1 Holway Point,
Machias, Maine 04654, U.S.A.

Spantech House
Lagham Road, South Godstone
Surrey RH9 8HB, U.K.

The publisher gratefully acknowledges the financial support of the
Alberta Foundation for the Arts, the *Alberta Historical Resources Foundation*
and the *Canada Council*.

Editorial and Publishing Consultant : George Melnyk
Design : George Allen
Production Assistance : Christine Spindler
Printed in Hong Kong

Canadian Cataloguing in Publication Data

Hildebrandt, Walter.
Brooks
A poem.
ISBN 1-896209-36-X
1. Brooks (Alta.) – Poetry. I. Tittenberger, Peter, 1952 – II.
Title.
PS8565.I4335B76 1996   C811'.54
PR9199.3.H54B76 1996   C95-911216-2

Again to Sarah and Mary

and to the memory of my parents

Gerhard and Ilse Hildebrandt

W.H.

To my family

P.T.

A photograph of the Krupp works or **AEG** yields almost nothing about these institutions. Reality proper has slipped into the functional. The reification of human relationships, the factory, let's say, no longer reveals these relationships. Therefore something has actually to be constructed, something artificial, something set up.

Bertolt Brecht

where water works
wonders

Structure

In the course of my walking the coping, not only did I walk that thing even when I was a manager, I walked it when it was full of water, looking for something to happen, maybe the coping was crumbling or something, and that was an exercise, that's where my nostalgia goes right out the window because if you're walking along this thing, and this thing is full of water, and it's moving at about three and a half feet per second average velocity, and the wind is blowing from the south, and you're looking down sixty feet ...

R.T. (Bob) White, local engineer

Post-structure

Thus, the relief and design of structures appears more clearly when content, which is the living energy of meaning, is neutralized. Somewhat like the architecture of an uninhabited or deserted city, reduced to its skeleton by some catastrophe of nature or art. A city no longer inhabited, not simply left behind, but haunted by meaning and culture.

J. Derrida

Irrigation first relied on the predictable flood cycles of major rivers in the Middle and Far East. With sufficient capital and labour flood irrigation was replaced by systems of regulated storage and distribution. In ancient civilizations a variety of irrigation works were developed including canals, artesian wells, elevated aqueducts and reservoirs. In almost all of these ancient civilizations the development of irrigation systems involved immense public works which included a centralized control over land, manpower and water rights.

After
    it was all
        over
we saw just how it us'to work

Commerce and Conquest in the Ancient World

In Africa and Europe this led to the distribution of irrigation technology east and west. Egyptian technology spread across North Africa, while the Roman carried techniques of water distribution into central Europe and Britain.

Native peoples practiced irrigation throughout South and Central America particularly in Argentina, Chile, Peru and Mexico. The Incas built canals, aqueducts and produced a wide variety of irrigation crops. Traces and remains of irrigation structures in Arizona and New Mexico testify to the presence of irrigation in prehistoric North America. In the Salt River Valley 1600 kilometers have been discovered. Some of these structures were reclaimed by Mormon settlers in the 1800s.

mountain

glacier thaw

let everything flow

In Canada the Dominion Experimental Farm system paid little attention to the possibility of irrigation in the Palliser triangle until after 1890. As the dry years accumulated threatening the destruction of vast rangelands many ranchers installed small systems on streams that could be easily directed to fertile haylands.

By 1890 enthusiasm grew into the investment possibilities of large ventures to bring extensive irrigation to the open prairie. Edward and Henry Maunsell ran the first major irrigation works in the Macleod area, turning water from the Oldman River on the Peigan Reserve onto more than five hundred acres in June 1870.

Even in times of crisis
capitalism
appropriated opposition
absorbed
the brooding Benjamin
combing the deserted
arcades of Paris
wondering
whether a theory of history
could be found to make fascism more visible
"the waking world towards which the past was dreaming"
in the drizzle
of the early morning streets
peering through cobwebs into the emptiness
of what was gone
pondering the dreams gone bad
the high hopes
of once new now lifeless
phalansteries
                              standing empty
their dreams there
for all to see
dreams to be documented

for all to see
novelty and repetition
anew
always a new
fantasy
                        alive
fantasy
                for sale
escaping
into the fantasy
getting away
from it all
closing eyes

escaping history
an awakening
a recognition
of what the structures
stood for
have become
                        for us
for them

The Brooks Aqueduct was
a testing ground
for new
and largely untried
systems

Column
girder
and brace
          were erected
     by stiff-leg derricks
travelling on skids
          and working backwards

my father
supplemented
a carpenter's wages
on weekends
                    out on the fields
                            opening the dykes
                                    letting the water flow

        out onto the land

turning

                        prairie desert into mud

did he think of prison camps
death sentences
out there on the land
where the water brought life?

Here warm winds blew
    from the mountains
        chinooks made
            brooks babble
                and I was born
                    Jan 2 1951

The Bassano Dam
      earthen and hollow reinforced concrete structure
      raised the Bow River
      forty feet
          to carry water
          across a shallow
              two mile
                    valley
first to use the
      hydrostatic catenary curve
     assumed the shape
      of a perfectly flexible container
      holding
          a flowing
             body
             of water

boys

      rode their ponies

  to the flume

       on hot summer days

   and cooled off

under the water

   spilling over

the side

   leaking from

     cracks

   cool and shady

        wet

       trickling

         down

local history

"Bloody liars" Bob White *said about*
          the boys who said
                    they dove
              through the siphon

      the only body ever seen
      go through
      a cancer victim jumped in
      his body found
      days later
      every bone in his body
      broken.

Forward
         (Ho!)

people came.   *The buffalo disappeared as*

                They left behind

                their bleached bones
                their wallows around huge buffalo rubbing stones
                and their dung
                        that pioneers collected
                        and burned as fuel.

was transient,   *The mark of the Indian*

                like themselves, erasing
                        their stories.

However it was
      the people,
      the farmers,
      the cowboys,
      the ranchers,
      the preachers,
      the Lord and Dukes,
      the remittance men
      and the ones
      who considered
      themselves
      "just common folk."

      who made the history.

They all cut a niche for themselves
in their adopted land and carved their
signatures into the land by word and action.

[Verbatim]

Native irrigation was being practiced in Kansas in the seventeenth century. A century later only ruins of the irrigation works were left. On the Blackfoot Reserve, the Department of Interior constructed irrigation works on the Bow River for 1,200 acres. Even the North-West Mounted Police had installed an irrigation system on their horse ranch at the Pincher Creek Post.

Does Anyone Tell All of Any Family History?

Here
in the local
family
                    histories
          the whole white story was told

          Progress

On the move again

Brooks Aqueduct Oct. 12, 1926

B-16

a giant

        centipede

                crawling

                        along

Welcome to Brooks

Brooks was named after Noel Edgell Brooks, a Canadian Pacific Railway divisional engineer at Calgary from 1903-1913. The signing of Treaty No. 7 with the Blood and Blackfoot [sic] Indians on Sept. 22, 1877 made the land in southern Alberta available for ranching. E.M. Crooker was the first citizen here in 1904 when he built a store. A townsite survey was registered in 1907 when the population was nine; a village was formed in 1910 and became a town the following year. The C.P.R. began constructing the irrigation systems in 1909 and in 1935 it was turned over to the water users and the Eastern Irrigation District was formed.

there is a fine new

                bandstand

where you might enjoy

                  your picnic lunch

and a five foot fence around the entire

                    museum

Thanks to Nova, an Alberta corporation

*unfortunately the checkerboard land
pattern was highly impractical
for the efficient distribution of water*

MAP

OF THE

EASTERN IRRIGATION DISTRICT

BROOKS — ALBERTA

SHOWING MAIN CANALS & RESERVOIRS

SCALE OF MILES
5 4 3 2 1 0 5 10

RG.16
RG.15
RG.17
TP. 25
TP. 24
RG.18
TP. 23
RG.14
TP. 22
RG.13
RG.12
RG.11
TP. 21
TP. 20
RG.18
TP. 19
TP. 18
TP. 17
RG.17
TP. 16
TP. 15
RG.16
TP. 14

RG.15 RG.14 RG.13 RG.12 RG.11.

RED DEER RIVER
BOW RIVER
CONTROL
GEM
BRIDGE
VERGER
MATZIWIN
MATZIWIN CREEK
GRAND FORKS
BASSANO
COUNTESS
CANADIAN PACIFIC CANAL
ROSEMARY
JOHN WARE DAM
DINOSAUR PARK
SECONDARY CANAL "A"
MAIN CANAL
BASSANO DAM
LATHOM
DUCHESS
TREE SPILLWAY
MILLICENT
PATRICIA
LECKIE
SPRING HILL
ROCK LAKE
PRINCESS
DENHART
SOUTHESK
SECONDARY
ONE TREE RESERVOIR
COWOKI RESERVOIR
CASSILS
BROOKS
TILLEY"B" RESERVOIR
MACBETH
BANTRY
TILLEY"A" (CAMPBELL) RESERVOIR
ANTELOPE CREEK CANAL
KITSIM CANAL
KITSIM RESERVOIR
LAKE NEWELL RESERVOIR
"J" RESERVOIR
TILLEY
MEZEKUM
HIGHWAY
BANTRY SUMMIT DRAIN
KINNVIE
RAINIER
SOUTH BANTRY SPILLWAY
ROLLING HILLS RESERVOIR
SCANDIA
SCANDIA BRIDGE
ROLLING HILLS
SECONDARY CANAL

The main building of the Brooks
and District Museum was built in 1974
in conjunction with the one
hundredth anniversary of the
Royal Canadian Mounted Police.

The museum is organized
to be a 'walk through the ages'

with displays presenting

> *the dinosaur;*
> *the Indian culture;*
> *the ranchers;*
> *the sheepmen;*
> *the homesteaders*
> *the farmers;*
> *the R.C.M.P.;*
> *the C.P.R.; and*
> *the E.I.D.*

as well as articles from the war years

The museum also houses
> *displays saluting*

> *the oil industry;*
> *the famous Pheasant Hatchery;*
> *pioneers of the area;*
> *including*
> *the Fourth Duke of Sutherland*
> *and a negro rancher*
> *John Ware;*
> *and professions of the past.*

[Verbatim]

It is the largest aqueduct
of its kind in the world
virtually an overhead river.

Brooks Bulletin 1914

The structure was put into operation early in 1914 and within twelve months serious trouble developed. At first there were small leaks but these soon developed into blow-outs.

A.S. Dawson

The number of water users was 67 and progress seemed assured through immediate development, however, will probably be retarded by conditions arising from the war.

                                        in a shack

ice two inches thick
grows on the walls

                                              in winter

                                        my mother
with me in her
                                              belly
washed floors
                                        for ladies
                              in town

living on the edge

U give it
a double take
cuz at first u can't
figure it out
looks like
a big grey mass of something
when u look south
of the highway
goin' to Calgary
like a tide
that should be movin'
but doesn't
u forget it
cuz u can't figure it out

What a big moment
glorious water
bubbling
effervescent
spray
rolling down
a concrete flume
out into the whole
network of dykes
all over the country
funneling water
out onto the sun-
warmed earth
turning
this sun-parched

desert land
into a place
where all kinds
of crops
could grow

Mud Mud Mud
(just like it rained
for 40 days and 40 nights)

THE ISSUE IS TO DIVIDE INTO TWO, DUPLICATE, DERIVE LANGUAGE WHICH IS A FILTER FOR THE BLOOD, AND THEN TO REPLENISH THOUGHT IN A PRECISE FLOW TO CONVERGE AGAIN ON LIFE HOW MUCH OF A COPY OF YOU I AM . . .

FRED WAH

Construction

to build an author
to carry me through
the story
to help me tell
about what I saw
the day I went back
to remember
the place
I was born

1985

looking
from the end like
it was an "H" with the top lopped off

and a sagging
middle
was the way it looked
as I drove up

it was useless
      this structure
            that looked like a grey tide
      from the Trans-Canada
         blocking the horizon
         (chain links)
            fenced now
               and dangerous

worn thru in places
      where the concrete
         just couldn't hold
            leaked thru
            all done
            all over

            an historic site

The structure
                    haunts
me/I
        can't get anything
                        to hold
    together

to stay
        still

            reaching in
                how little we know
                    across
                            the generations
        lives
            growing
                        out
                    landscapes no one can walk

what can you read
  in black and white
      in faded bent   faces

  there's too much
      my father
        wouldn't tell me
  about the prisons
      the trials
  the spying missions

      he told my brother and me
there was too much
      that was
        different
  too much we couldn't
      understand

44

no context

    for what the communists did

he never trusted socialists anywhere

     almost voted for Blakeney once

we almost persuaded him

    he said it was time to tell us

the concrete crumbles

    you can hardly save

       a fraction

   of what goes by

     every second

the basic structures

        stand

         still

  the imagination

    gives back

  what's on the surface

     floating

only fragments
        that once held together
    pieces
        pictures
                    printed
                        pages
        words
            leaking
                out
                    of the stories
        between the cracks
                that need to be told
    to those who still
                    condemn

these stories
victims seldom tell
        afraid they won't be understood
        afraid that nothing will fit
        afraid they can't explain
        the broader picture
        afraid they're guilty

how one gets swept along
how little choice there is
for resistance
amid massacres and hangings
history begins
when your brothers are sent to Siberia
when you're drafted into the Red Army
where do loyalties lie
for those that Stalin killed
there was no structure for his story
you don't last long standing still
in the current
you get carried away
one day you march one way
the next another
there were only big rivers
no smaller streams
you had no choice
nothing seemed man-made
nothing simple as
moving water thru canals
onto fields where crops waited to grow
there was only fear

the fear that someone would hold a gun to your head
as you lay in the ditch exhausted
the fear that someone
would say "Get up or I'll shoot"
that much he told us that much he said
he said that at the time
he didn't care if he was shot or not
you just keep walking somehow
in the sea of prisoners
and some are lost
in the ditches at the side of the road
some are lost along the way
you join the flow or fall away
lost in the run-off
one day you march one way
the next day the other
you can't explain these things easily
there is no structure no narrative
to hold these stories yet
those who held power
made sure there was one story

the story of progress
that was for the good of all
even if all had not been heard
imagine two big rivers running
across the land
two big rivers you wanted to leave
them both behind
no one would walk away
there was no grey
there were no streams
there was either/or
there was no and/but
imagine a military trial
where they didn't believe
you were who you said you were
and what does it mean to say who you are
where will that put you
my father was asked to prove
he was a German
or be executed
he was asked by the officer in command
to say anything to make them believe
he was one of them
and my father a student of literature
mentioned the name of little known
Mennonite writer not a mainstream
writer not a writer you would

know if you weren't a German
he mentioned this vernacular
writer Fritz Reuter
and the officer let him go
no Russian would know the
works of a Mennonite who
wrote in the vernacular
they let him go for knowing
the name of a minor writer
a small voice in the wilderness
they let him go they let him go
and then the British let him go
the Russians and the Germans and the British let him go
and this is all we have
droplets really
so little to build anything around
nothing to move into

it needed beginnings
new beginnings there were
not enough voices to make a history
just a few letters from the old country
the last letters from his brothers and sisters
just these little bits
the structure wouldn't hold
couldn't contain

the love of literature the love of work
to make the water flow
along the man made channels
to places where it could be useful
to make things do what you want them to
not to be swept along
you could make choices
you could dream out on the prairie
you could dream big dreams
you could dream of making new rivers
you could dream small dreams
you could dream of building a home
you could dream of freedom
you could dream out on the prairie
in the sun
you could start

                              begin again

they didn't ask who you were
out here in the sun
the water moving slowly through
these ditches when you opened the gates
the water moving slowly
Being let out onto the land
Being born
            Becoming

CPR Crews

THEY HAS THESE WORK CAMPS
THEY CALLED THEM
I CAN REMEMBER
I WAS ALWAYS FASCINATED BY THEM
THEY HAD WOODEN
LIKE CARAVANS
ON WHEELS PULLED WITH HORSES
AND SOME OF THESE CAMPS HAD UP TO TWO HUNDRED HORSES
AND THESE WAGON TRAINS
AND THERE THEY HAD THEIR MATERIAL IN ONE
AND THEIR EQUIPMENT
AND THEY WOULD HAVE THEIR SLEEPING QUARTERS
AND THEY ALSO HAD THEIR KITCHEN.

AND EACH ONE OF THEM
HAD A CHINESE COOK
WITH A PIGTAIL.

By the late 1890s a group of men led by William Pearce, a civil engineer and irrigation theoretician, had begun to lobby actively for federal involvement in irrigation development, much on the model that was emerging in the United States. Pearce and his irrigation allies were strongly opposed by both the CPR, who feared the spread of rumours that the west was unsuited to settlement, and by the major ranchers who dreaded farmer blockades of the streams once completely open to stock watering.

Western agitation for federal intervention followed the American approach:

1. government assumption of title to all surface water,
2. extensive government surveys of all water resources and storage and distribution sites,
3. stringent regulations for equitable water distribution.

standin' out on that land
dry as a bone
parched   flaked   cracked
        in patterns
                of squares and circles
        crevices
                where water disappeared
        when it rained
                rock hard in spots
        a dream
                of movin' a river over
        this valley

    in summer
                spoken words
        were few
                but the plan
                was exciting

                        said they'd build
        an aqueduct

Log S = X(M) + log V - 2/3 log R) - 6.00 *

low slope

high friction

compounded by cross-struts

impinged

upon the flow

* **Professor Fidler's formula**

R is hydraulic mean radius

V is velocity

S is grade

X is friction factor

M is friction factor depending on shape

1919	Wages for teamsters & labourers = $4.00 / 10 hour day
1920	$4.50 / 10 hour day
1921	$3.50 / 10 hour day
1922-25	$3.00 / 10 hour day

Tonight
      by the edge of a lake
                         the surface
                                   still

On this calm late sunlit dusk
                   so much
          can't be seen

I look to tell you
what is held in these waters
And my mind
          desperate
as if too much is lost in storms past
                   and to come

Your grandfather
      in my eyes
        near nightfall
            the ultramarine of the sea
                and the grey flow of the Volga

Your grandmother
      in my laugh
      strange language
            the blue Prussian mountains
               the bandstand music
                   in Bad Herzberg

hands
      that first held me
        carried me along

dreams
    surrounded by darkness
        made us believe
            the impossible
  "make us believe"
       the broken begged
  "make us believe"
  give us a voice
       show us our place
  give us meaning
     any meaning
     start
         the journey
         remembering the words
      dreaming
          in the heart of darkness
      dreaming
        out of darkness

lookin'

        for an idea

for a fast and cheap

          method

of buildin' forms
over which large animal skins
      could be stretched
(elephant and hippopotamus)
when he came up with the idea
    of spraying
rough frames with
      Portland cement
a thin skin of gunnite

At the discharge end of this is a nozzle, to which another and smaller hose supplies water, also under pressure. The hydration thus takes place while all the materials are in motion, and the resulting mixture, leaving the nozzle, is "shot" upon the surface to be coated, or into the interstices of any aggregate. The mortar issues from the nozzle orifice in the form of a spray ... leaving a thin film of fine cement mortar to serve as a plastic base in which they finally become embedded. The mixture is then built up upon the film to any thickness desired.

Anonymous

The Cement Gun, Gunnite and their Uses

... "Angelus Novas".

An angel is presented in it
who looks as if he were about
to move away from something
at which he is staring. His
eyes are wide open, mouth agape,
wings spread. The angel of
history must look like that.
His face turned toward
the past. Where a chain
of events appears to us, he
sees one single catastrope
which relentlessly piles wreckage
upon wreckage, and hurls them
before his feet ... the storm
[from Paradise] drives him irresistably
into the future to which his
back is turned, while the pile
of debris before him grows
toward the sky. That which
we call progress is this storm.

Walter Benjamin on Paul Klees' painting

there were always
the dreams
of making something from nothing
making the land productive
making money out of anything and everything
any place could be made bountiful
all that was needed was water
to make things grow
the land so barren
and the people who came had so many dreams

dreams of a new future / a better future
a new Jerusalem / a new start

all those engineers with ideas
and money piles of money
technology know-how
cement and steel
electricity
cranes and winches
transportation
railways to move
material
to resist corrosion

and erosion
the rusting the wearing away of the topsoil
blowing around
and discoveries everyday more discoveries
to make things better
and bigger
bigger and better
an overhead river
along a bed of cement
the engineers had thought of

                                everything

people here were optimistic about their future
not the past the future
hope in the future
furthering ourselves / bettering ourselves
the past was war poverty depression
the Indians lived in the past
the future was for the believers
the believers in vision
in technology
to make things better
and bigger

the trouble with history was that it was full of failures

now we can see
what's left
what was left out
what you could not predict
the materials that let you down
the miscalculation
what the optimists left out
for history
                    to remind
us about questions that
couldn't be asked

                            at the time
that were never asked
of those who told them
you could build a river
the way of the future
cement   steel   electricity   railways
ploughed the future forgot the land
the people the rain ice and snow
the water the power of the land
if only you could sell them
on the future
again

it was simple
the promised land
everyone wants / a future
we'll build a better tomorrow
these guys can sell
the technology
sell the river
this overhead river
the wave of the future
down the river
everyone wanted to believe
in money
travelling the river of tomorrow
to share the wealth
to believe

quiet
                    calm

crumbling slowly
history stands so still
staring
the concrete
                         daydreams

of Paradise
Paradise
they offered

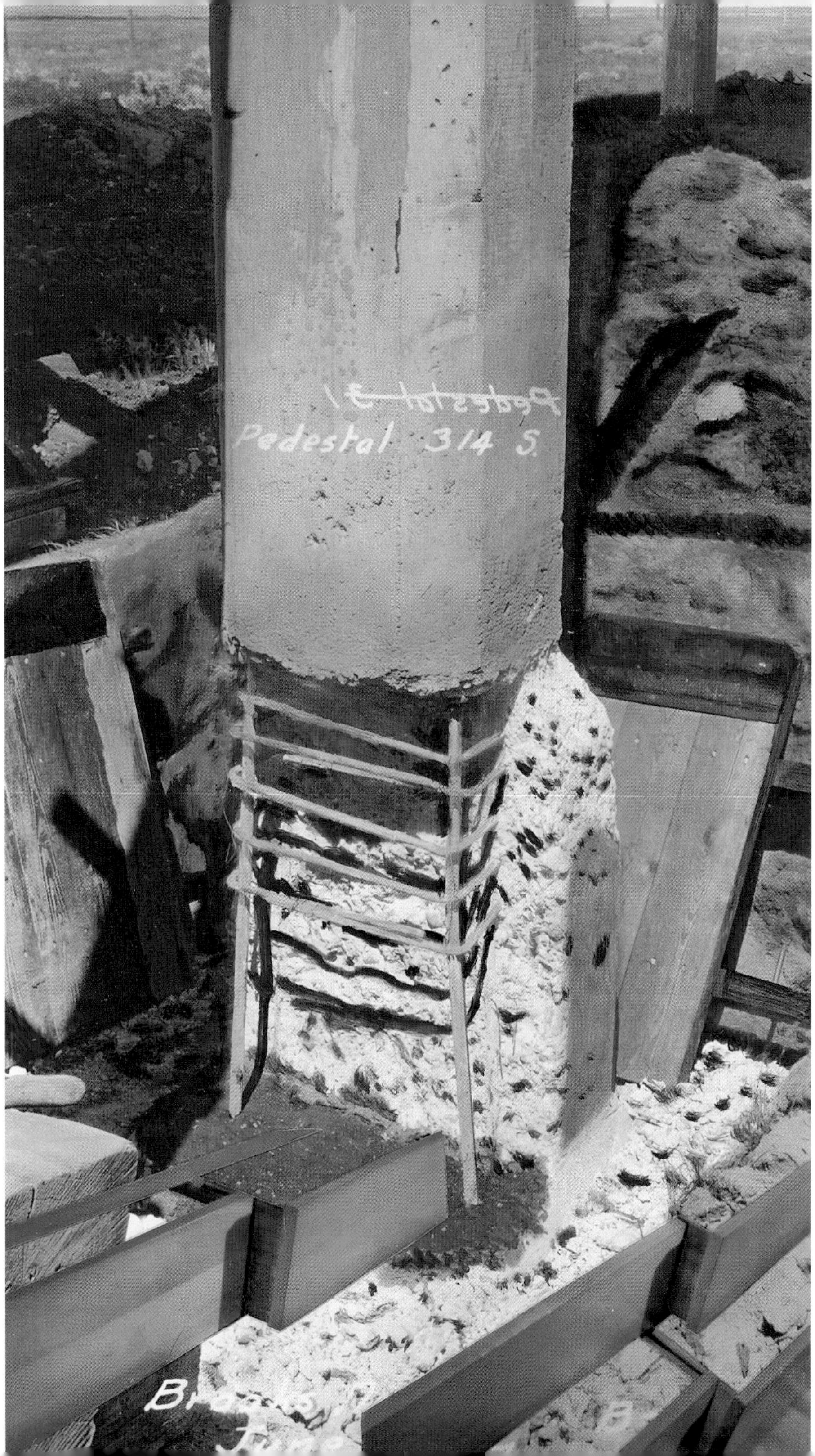
Pedestal 314 S.

1941

bearded
bent
almost broken
he shuffled
out
of prison
in Nowo-Sibirsk
more like a corpse than a person
his feet swollen
people in the street
cleared an arch
around him
he could hardly stand
and had to sit and rest every few steps

1943

he was called to the front

ANTELOPE CREEK SYPHON, Apr. 18, 19

7'-6" WOOD STAVE PIP

No. B-642

FISHING

... ANOTHER LITTLE ANTIDOTE AS YOU
MENTION ABOUT THE THING, THE
AQUEDUCK WAS THAT EACH FALL
WHEN THEY DRAINED THE IRRIGATION CANAL
THERE WAS ALWAYS QUITE A CROWD WOULD GATHER
AT THE AQUEDUCK
THE PLACE WHERE IT WENT UNDER THE RAILROAD.
THIS WOULD TRAP ALL THE FISH
THAT WERE IN THE CANAL
THEY'D GET TRAPPED
IN THE PART UNDERNEATH THE RAILWAY
WHEN THE WATER WAS ALL SHUT OFF ON BOTH SIDES
AND IT QUIT RUNNING
THEN THEY'D OPEN TWO BIG STEEL DOORS AND
THE NATIVES AROUND BROOKS THERE
WOULD JUST GET SACKS OF FISH OUT THERE
WHITEFISH MOSTLY
THAT WERE TRAPPED IN THERE WHEN THE WATER WAS SHUT OFF.

SO THAT WAS ALWAYS QUITE AN OCCASION
IN THE FALL
WHEN THE WATER WAS SHUT OFF
TO GET THE FISH OUT OF THERE.

... AQUEDUCK SOUP

nothing dramatic
like the Passiac here
just these personal stories
men working
water stagnant
on the really hot days
only insects broke the surface calm
the man-made here as everywhere
seemed beyond control
technology, the CPR
you could never tell
for sure if it was working
for or against the farmer, the labourer
the same everywhere
being told it was all for the best

Well and
        they brought
out these big Jesus
                concrete making machines
most massive
                  undertaking
       of its kind
     tons of cement
them big buggers sure poured out
lots of cement
        1000 men
      worked 30 years
     to build the whole
       darn thing up

The first years of the EID were filled with buoyant optimism. Land values were reduced to a fifth of the CPR costs while water rates were increased. In the first four years the system ran at a profit that allowed them to leave the CPR's $300,000.00 grant virtually untouched.

The books showed a profit and that the irrigated acreage had been increased from 90,000 to 134,000 between 1935 and 1938. The District introduced new electric water pumps and built several new reservoirs. Hail insurance, and a co-operative livestock venture added to the sense of security, but it was ignoring dire problems that would eventually destroy its cash flow.

Yeah
        the CPR
got lots
          for buildin'
the railway
          an' this here land
was preat' near useless
so in this part
         of the country
they took a big shit kickin' first
tryin' to make the land bountiful
but they got
         smart
 and eventually
         got most of it back
by
    soakin'
       the farmer

At his trial
he recited
"Da Drom" / Der Traum / The Dream
and the officer said
that no Jew could do that
the terrible difference between life and death

Men like Carl Anderson and Bill Sheldrake for the local contract holders, George Walker for the CPR and O.S. Longman for the Government became intimately involved in developing the idea of an independent, owner-operator irrigation district. It was a radical solution and in the end it was the farmers themselves who had to be convinced that it would be to their benefit to be burdened with an operation that had cost the CPR so much. In 1939 the railway decided that the eastern section should be sloughed off to a farmer operated co-operative if they could be convinced to take it. It became increasingly clear that the company was preparing to rid themselves of the district at almost any cost.

See
they charged
                    heavy
for the leases
'til the farmers got mad
and stood up to the bastards
organized
                    'n
got'em to reduce
                    the charges
then bought them out
                    and made it pay

                    for a couple of years

frogs
not known in this land before
sat around pools
pilgrims along the canal
croaked for rain all night long
praying for the miracle
singing in gratitude
to replenish the pools that dried so fast in the heat of day

Nothing the company did actually relieved the farmers of the original capital debt. With the onset of the Depression, farm abandonment exceeded settlement, many who stayed simply became subsistence farmers, the EID's operating revenue shrank accordingly. The company became anxious to divest itself of the system.

dreamed
on hot
days
of water
moving
so slowly
down
along the canals
and the grass
growing along the edge
soaking it all up
flowing steadily
rising
sinking
in the wet
ground
overflowing

Once More 'Round the Block

Nova, an Alberta corporation

there is a fine new

                bandstand

where you might enjoy

                    your picnic lunch

and a five foot fence around the entire

                        museum

"inverted siphon"
        ya ever heard of that
to carry water
        under the track
and back up
        yep
            believe it
                or not

Break-up began

      concrete

           weakened

      water seeped in

        to cracks

   and froze

        as blizzards

followed

        Chinooks

nothin' really could be done 'gainst the elements

In the end

        I

understand

        it was all

a big

       mis-calculation

     the mathematical formula
     called for it
       to be built
          at a certain angle

Well and they just couldn't
do it that way
the engineer fucked it up
proper design didn't work

     too much

          resistance

water ran

     down the flume

too much wear

       against the concrete

see

            legs

still

            look

strong

        but the rest

    of its

        all gibbled up

    in the end

      I guess

        it just couldn't hold

It just

    wouldn't

hold

    bugger all

sad

      as the water

ran

   'n

      really

wrecked

      the whole

dam thing

      busted

all over

the wind
                    just
        whistles
along the decrepit
                old flume
and between
            the concrete legs
                        stained with
                            gunnite

kinda

        rough

    the patch jobs

        kept falling

                to pieces

we used

              this mixture - gunnite

    s'posed to be

           best kinda stuff

    available

but water kept

    comin' thru

trickle

    at first

but soon there

    were just gaping

holes

    sorry

te see all the work go

    for not

Poor gravel
        some said
    contractor cut corners
            but the alkaline soil
yea it was the alkaline
        in the soil
                attacked
                        the cement
                fine for soil around Calgary
    but
                broke
                    down
                            completely

out here

        leaks
                    caulked
            with oakum
                    and petrolastic

Yea
The whole thing just stood there
a tired zygal
the down side
a big fat C.P.R. capitalist
on sturdy legs
with his low slung gut

CPR

locals called the railway
            "Canadian Pathetic"
rumour had it
condemned cement
poured into the flume
"the work was not without its troubles"

Well after a while
u just couldn't
fix it
it was no good

cement crumblin'
away

ree-bar stikin' out
all over

it just couldn't hold
water

they had to shut her down

too dangerous to crawl on even

Weight
                              just got
too heavy
                              on the linin'
an' just like
                              an ulcer
perforated
                              the membrane

legs stayed sturdy tho
but like I say the linin'
                              gave way
the pull down
                              ward

you know
gravity
screwed it
all up

all over
stories come from the work
        it was hard to make them
    for people to see
    all those guys
    who once had names
    allota the stories were just there
              for themselves
    few remember
        what it was like
    and stories ran out
one of the college boys
    who visited here
        said he was
interested in what was gone
        "kenosis" he called it
         enclosures leaking
    history
        fences
          falling
            apart

        spillage

beads
        formed
into tiny streams
    running
            down
soaked
            in a cold sweat
    the bundle holder
        dreamed
                a dream
        where guns lay rusted
prairie grasses
            growing
                in and around them
        reminders
they deserted the land
    leaving tracks
                abandoned

sagging telegraph lines
        elevators
    falling down
                nesting places
                        now
for swallows
                        coming back
    an' buffalo
                        coming back
in waves
            returning
        spreading out
                over the land

giddy
       blue-prints in hand
             engineers enthralled
couldn't wait to dam
             more rivers
taken by their own
                    technology
heady with their own
               power
      to build the Aswan
"the worst ecological mistake of mankind"
    grotesque drainage problems
    poisoning salts
           silting reservoirs
    extinct fish

    bringing water to poorly drained land
       the huge fascination
       watching in awe
           the immensity
       of all the concrete
         holding up
         so much

Now these fuckin' bastards
  these pirates
    raiders
    wanna
   gouge new channels
    chased treasures west
     into the sea
       then north

wanna redraw maps
    move the last fresh reservoirs
 of water
      for opulent artificial
       California gardens

  the Rocky Mountain Trench
huge diversions
    for ornamental deserts

feeding colossal false-fronted failures

And here this aqueduct
   skeleton of a dream

  they'll try it
   just when no one thought they could

the old house
       I looked for
              is gone

and coming home
       you said there was something
          I could add

on the way to my sister's
       Mary sleeps beside us
it's here
        Sarah
poems
        writing
   run, run
        run
          run
            a
              w
                a
                   y

       grace
slick
       you know
         all for u
           just U
   carried away
          running on

"Freiheit Muß Hier Nicht Enden"

In Canada
> *Mennonites*
>> *conscientious objectors*
> *worked the beet fields*
>> *"Arbeit Macht Frei"*

>> *anti-Semitism*
> *freedom must not end here*

>> *in Auschwitz-Birkenau*
> *ideas of wealth*
>> *to think*
>> *to believe*
>>> *this warehouse*
>>> *of gold fittings*

>>> *Kanada*
>>> *in ashes*

water to bathe in
water to heal the cracked skin of the earth
tears to mend the scarred lives
this ancient medicine to cleanse the mind
to see clearly again
warm rains
diving to escape enemies
surviving above and below the surface
moving on
building the new onto the old
serene at the edge at the end
in this ocean of grass
lying under the dome of this huge glorious prairie sunset

drained by the middle
    the flow stopped short
        of the expected
                ending
      confusion
          for those who wanted
         everything
            complete
        in a brilliant
           finish

So many ways
to make it work
to let the story of the father
speak for itself
to let the structure stand
without a sense of the passage of time
let the story flow
without interruption
to disrupt the main point
with interjections
that cause problems
like Charles Noble
out there on
the land
in his tractor
thinking of Peirce
furthering the Sign
Grounding rainbows
farming the Interpretant
referring the Object
forwards and backwards
without end

what's all that got to do with it
    politics
        nobody liked the politics
  wanting a story without politics
    to make the past seem
        like it couldn't have happened
        any other way
    let people believe
        in the expected
    let things go on
        "naturally"
    the way they're supposed to

that's what has to change
    nothing's as it's supposed to be
the unexpected is everywhere
    everything is man made
  unpredictable
    it's hard to say

what will happen
    which wall is about to come down
what technology will promise
    which one will break
        down next
which one will be
        bad for you
    you can't have a nice beginning
        middle and end
     you're just not going to get it
      here where I was born
    everything seems
        to rush in together
       all at once
     I can't keep things
        separate

and order them carefully

in compartments

        to fit

    the expectations of

    a nice story

it just didn't happen

      that way

    being what I was

growing up where I did

    confused about what it meant

to be a German

    the son of an immigrant

      people had done

        such horrible things

      being treated

        suspiciously

      by neighbours

        whose relatives

      died in the war

and my father
never wanting
          to tell me much
to tell me anything
          to add
     to the confusion
of why it was difficult for him
          at the university
     where they wouldn't acknowledge
          his education
          in world literature
from a German university
          in the Soviet Union
had to start over again
          here

even if you had the papers
we wouldn't recognize
that here
you'll have to start over again
in the middle
start over again
in the middle of your life
go back over the old ground
where you first saw the light
where you first learned
to stand
for yourself
on the prairie
go over the old stories

here
where irrigation
        let people think
they could start
            at the end
        in a desert
            what was seen
        at the end of the earth
            round
                in a circle
it didn't seem to matter
            where I put
                everything / anything
a circle
            not a line
where you began in the end
            or the middle
                for that matter

things still rushed
  into and across
the main story
  I was trying to tell
to start with ...
    about the aqueduct
  progress
against the grain
    me the historian
    explaining
    this attempt to make things better
  after they got worse
    in a circle
  over and over
      starting over
    returning to the birthplace
    where it all began
      beginnings
    everywhere
      without end

I started with the past
and in the past
building on the past
changing the past
by adding to it
by telling my own story
I can't look at the past the same anymore
I've changed the past
left it open

rewritten the history
of what it was like
to be born on the prairie

and what if
everyone
wrote to change
the past
to change the story
that is told about you
to change history
change the past
to change the present
so everyone
can start up
let it all...

begin again

ACKNOWLEDGEMENTS

I wrote a draft of this long poem in 1988 after a visit to Brooks in search of the house I was born in. There have been many reworkings of the material and I would like to thank the following people who made comments on the manuscript over the years: David Arnason, Ken Hughes, Per Brask, Birk Sproxton, Charles Noble, and especially Don Kerr, who I believe read each of the many versions. Thanks to Dr. Sarah McKinnon, the curator of Gallery IC03 at the University of Winnipeg where *Brooks: Coming Home* was on display from January 12 to February 6, 1993. I am particularly grateful to Peter Tittenberger who joined the project to produce the visual text: the collages and tinted photographs. Also many thanks to Ashis Gupta and George Melnyk for their enthusiastic support for this project. Thanks to Gerry Bander and the staff of the Eastern Irrigation District in Brooks for assisting with the location and identification of the map and photographs. I would also like to acknowledge the Alberta Foundation for the Arts for a grant that allowed me the time to work on the manuscript. A portion of this manuscript was published in *blue buffalo* no. 12 :1, winning first prize in a contest entitled *Public History / Private History.*

PHOTOGRAPHIC SOURCES

GAI : Glenbow Alberta Archives
PAA : Provincial Archives of Alberta
EID : Eastern Irrigation District Library

Front cover	GAI	NA–4389–31
Back Cover	GAI	NA–2622–65
Page 6	PAA	P_820
Page 13	Collection of Walter Hildebrandt	
Page 19	GAI	NA–2622–65
Page 21	GAI	NA–2622–63
Page 23	EID	
Page 30	GAI	NA–4389–31
Page 53	GAI	NA–206–21
Page 61	GAI	NA–2622–68
Page 63	EID	
Page 69	GAI	NA–4389–36
Page 71	GAI	NA–4389–16
Page 73	GAI	NA–206–20
Page 76	GAI	NA–5200–46
Page 90	*Brooks Bulletin*	
Page 106	EID	
Page 118	EID	

ENDNOTES

Material on the following pages has been quoted directly and the sources of these direct quotations are as follows: page 27, *Brooks: Beautiful – Bountiful* by Eva Delday, Friesen and Sons, 1975; page 36 is from an unpublished handout for the Brooks Museum; page 52, page 72 quoted in *The Brooks Aqueduct: A Technological and Engineering History 1912 – 79,* by David Finch, Manuscript Report Series No. 360, Canadian Parks Service, Environment Canada, 1988.

Other sources consulted for historical background were: *Tapping the Bow* by Renie Gross and Lea Nicoll Kramer, Friesen and Sons, 1985 and *Cadillac Desert: The American West and Its Disappearing Water* by Marc Reisner, Douglas and McIntyre, 1986.